Are We *Good* Enough for Liberty?

Are We *Good* Enough for Liberty?

By Lawrence W. Reed

FOUNDATION FOR ECONOMIC EDUCATION
Atlanta

JAMESON BOOKS, INC.
Ottawa, Illinois

1-800-960-4FEE (4333)

Foundation for Economic Education
30 S. Broadway
Irvington, New York 10533

Foundation for Economic Education
260 Peachtree St. NW
Suite 2200
Atlanta, GA 30303

ISBN-10: 0-89803-174-5
ISBN-13: 978-0-89803-174-4

Find FEE online at:
Facebook.com/FEEonline
Twitter.com/FEEonline (@feeonline)

For single and bulk mail orders, contact Jameson Books, Inc.
P.O. Box 738
Ottawa, IL 61350
800-426-1357
See bulk discounts coupon on the final page of this book.

Cover and text design by Charles King, ckmm.com

16 15 14 13 5 4 3 2 1

Printed in the United States of America

Contents

Foreword

This small book conveys a *very* big message: character makes all the difference in the world. You are personally in charge of your own character and are in a position to have a considerable influence on the character of others by your example. If you have a conscience, this should matter a great deal to you. If you value liberty, you must understand that character is an indispensable ingredient—a necessary pre-condition—for a free society.

I'll venture one step further and offer this thought, upon which I have elaborated in other places and publications: *no people who lost their character kept their liberties.* That may be the most important lesson from the last five thousand years of human history.

In my visits to communist countries before the collapse of the Soviet Union, I witnessed the power of character as it eroded an evil system. In Poland in 1986 I met secretly with a very brave couple, Zbigniew and Sofia Romaszewski. They had only lately been released from prison for running an illegal underground radio station that broadcasted a message of liberty for Poland.

"How did you know if people were listening?" I asked. Sofia answered, "We could only broadcast eight to ten minutes at a time before moving on to another place to stay ahead of the police. One night we asked people to blink their lights if they believed in freedom. We then went to the window and for hours, all of Warsaw was blinking." The Iron Curtain fell in Poland and across Eastern Europe in 1989, in large part because of such heroes with character. They never gave up working for what they knew was right.

That story is the genesis of the Foundation for Economic Education's (FEE) ambitious "Blinking Lights Project," launched in the spring of 2013. It aims to inspire and educate young people in the principles of character, liberty, and entrepreneurship—and how those three critical elements of a free society are inextricably linked. Character comes first and makes liberty possible, and one of the highest and most noble callings of a responsible adult in a free society is to be an honest entrepreneur who creates value, employs people, and solves problems.

This book is one component of FEE's Blinking Lights Project. Another is the wide distribution of the 2006 film "Amazing Grace." In coming months and years, the project will also involve seminars and other publications focused on the themes of character, liberty, and entrepreneurship. You can learn more about it by visiting http://FEE.org/blp. We hope you will join us in this endeavor by attending a seminar or sponsoring a student, by distributing our materials including copies of this book, and by contributing financially if you can.

Former British Prime Minister William Ewart Gladstone once said, "We look forward to the day when the power of love replaces the love of power.

Only then will the world know the blessings of peace." Those words constitute both a warning and a promise. Gladstone was essentially calling us all to lives of character. Do we have the courage and the wisdom to put character at the top of our priorities? I dread the consequences if the answer proves to be "No."

—Lawrence W. Reed, President
Foundation for Economic Education
Newnan, Georgia
July 2013

Liberty and Character:
The Indispensable Connection

(This is an expanded edition of what was originally delivered as a Commencement address in 2006 at the Thomas Jefferson Independent Day School in Joplin, Missouri, and in 2007 at the Brookfield Academy in Brookfield, Wisconsin. Mr. Reed has since delivered versions of this address before audiences all over the world.)

In 1987 something quite remarkable happened in the little town of Conyers, Georgia. When school officials there discovered that one of their basketball players who had played 45 seconds in the first of the school's five post-season games had actually been scholastically ineligible, they returned the state championship trophy their beloved Rockdale Bulldogs had just won a few weeks before. If they had simply kept quiet, probably no one else would have ever known about it and they could have retained the trophy.

To their eternal credit, the team and the town, dejected though they were, rallied behind the school's decision. Coach Cleveland Stroud said, "We didn't know he was ineligible at the time . . . but you've got to do what's honest and right and what the rules say. I told my team that people forget the scores of the games; *they don't ever forget what you're made of.*"

In the minds of most, it didn't matter that the championship title was forfeited. The coach and the team were still champions—in more ways than one. Could *you* have mustered the courage under similar circumstances to do as they did?

Commencement addresses at both high schools and colleges are full of paeans and platitudes that reduce to one cliché: "You are the future." Well, that's an important point but it's also something we already know because it's pretty self-evident, wouldn't you say? So I'll not tell you in a dozen different ways that the future is yours. You should already know that. I have a different message.

I want to talk to you about one thing that is more important than all the good grades you've earned, more important than all the high school and college degrees you'll accumulate, and indeed, more important than all the knowledge you'll ever absorb in your lifetimes. It's something over which every responsible, thinking adult has *total*, personal control and yet millions of people every year sacrifice it for very little. It will not only define and shape your future; it will put both a concrete floor under it and an iron ceiling over it. It's what the world will remember you for more than probably anything else. It's not your looks, it's not your talents, it's not your ethnicity and ultimately, it may not even be anything you ever say. What is this incredibly powerful thing I'm talking about? In a word, it's *character.*

You need to know that character is indispensable to a successful career, a happy life, and a clear conscience. Without it, *you ain't goin' anywhere*. I recommend that you bulk up on it; if you do, you'll be amazed at how most if not all of the other elements of a successful career will eventually fall into place. On frequent occasions it will more than compensate for mistakes and shortcomings in other areas.

From an employer's perspective, Warren Buffett makes the point plainly: "In looking for someone to hire, you look for three qualities: integrity, intelligence, and energy. But the most important is integrity [a synonym for character], because if they don't have that, the other two qualities, intelligence and energy, are going to kill you."

Character is what the coach and the players in Conyers, Georgia, possessed. And what an example they set! Many of us will be telling that story for a long, long time. People with character set a standard and exert a pressure on others to strive to meet it.

A Poor But Honest Man

Here's another example from personal experience: In my travels to some eighty-one countries around the world, I have witnessed many sterling examples of personal character (as well as the startling lack of it), but this is one of the best.

In 1989 I visited Cambodia with my late friend Dr. Haing S. Ngor (who won an Academy Award for his role in the movie "The Killing Fields"). In advance of the trip, there was considerable local press attention because I was rustling up donated medical supplies to take with me to give to a hospital in the capital, Phnom Penh. A woman from a local church who saw the news stories called and explained that a few years before, her church had helped Cambodian families who had escaped from the Khmer Rouge communists and resettled in the town where I was living at the time—Midland, Michigan. The families had moved on to other locations in the United States but stayed in touch with the woman who called me and other friends they had made in Midland.

The woman—Sharon Hartlein is her name—said she had told her Cambodian friends about my pending visit. Each family asked if I would take letters with cash enclosed to their relatives in Cambodia. I said yes.

Two of the families were in Phnom Penh and easy to find, but one was many miles away in Battambang. Going there would have involved a train ride, some personal risk, and a lot of time it turned out I didn't have. I was advised in any event *not* to return with any money. If I couldn't locate any of the families I was told to just give the cash to any needy Cambodian I could find (and they were *everywhere!*).

On the day before my return home, when I realized I just wasn't going to make it to Battambang, I approached a man in tattered clothes whom I had seen several times in the hotel lobby. He always smiled and said hello, and spoke enough English so that we could briefly converse. He, like most Cambodians at that time, was practically penniless.

You can be sure that the status of his 401K plan never came up in our conversations.

"I have an envelope with a letter and $200 in it, addressed to a family in Battambang. Do you think you could get it to them?" I asked. "If you do, I want you to keep $50 of it for your trouble and expense and give the rest to the family." He consented, and we said goodbye. I assumed I would never hear anything of what had become of either him or the money.

Several months later, I received an excited call from Sharon. She said she had just received a letter from the Cambodians in Virginia whose family in Battambang that envelope was intended for. When she read it on the phone, I couldn't help but shed a few tears. The letter read, "Thank you for the *two hundred dollars*!"

That poor man found his way to Battambang, and he not only didn't keep the $50 I plainly offered, he somehow found a way to pay for the $10 train ride himself. Now, that is *character*! I think I would probably trust my life in his hands, even though I never got to know him and didn't ask him for his address.

To help us understand what character is, let me tell you what the absence of it looks like. Sadly, evidence of a lack of character is in abundance these days.

In 1995 students on the quiz team at Steinmetz High School in Chicago made national news when it was discovered that they had cheated to win a statewide academic contest. With the collaboration of their teacher, they worked from a stolen copy of a test to look up and memorize the correct answers in advance. Perhaps worse than the initial deed was the attitude of the same students five years later, expressed in *The New York Times* by one of them this way: "Apologize for what? I would do it again."

What a contrast to the values on display in the Conyers story—and even more so the Cambodian one! No one would say that the teacher or those students in Chicago exhibited character in the positive sense that I am using the term here. Assume for a moment that the Chicago students had never been caught. Knowing everything else that I've told you in these true stories, which group of students would you most want to be like—the ones in Conyers who walked away from a trophy or the ones in Chicago who cheated to win a contest? If you said Conyers, then you have a conscience. You have character, and hopefully a lot of it. And you know something of the inestimable value of being able to look back on your life some day and know that you tried hard in every circumstance to do the right thing.

I love the words of the Apostle Paul, in prison, shortly before he was martyred. It is recorded in Scripture as II Timothy 4:7: "I have fought the good fight, I have finished the race, I have kept the faith." He had character, even in the midst of extreme adversity. If he had sacrificed it for short-term, selfish gain, all his good words and deeds would hardly carry the weight they do today, nearly twenty centuries later.

Where Does Character Come From?

A deficit of character shows up every time somebody who knows the right thing to do neither defends it nor does it because doing so might mean a little discomfort or inconvenience. When I was president of the Mackinac Center for Public Policy in Michigan, from 1987 to 2008, I worked in the field of public policy. The job brought me into frequent contact with legislators, congressmen, and candidates for public office. Far too many times I heard words like these: "I know you're right, but I can't say so or vote that way because I won't get reelected."

You can blame a politician when he behaves that way but don't forget the voters who put him in that spot. I see character deficits every time I see people pressuring the government to give them something at the expense of others, something which they know in their very gut should come instead from their own efforts and merit. I see it every time voters reward a corrupt officeholder with praise and re-election. Effectively bought and paid for with other people's money, they compromise their integrity and independence for a handout, a subsidy, a special privilege.

Perhaps we should ask, "Where does character come from?" or, putting the question slightly differently, "Why is it that when we speak of character, we all seem to know what it is that we're talking about?" Theologians and philosophers can speak to this much better than I can. But I will say this: There is something in the way that we humans are wired. Down deep within us we have a sense of what is right and what is wrong, what is good and what is bad. And when we ignore our wiring, something within us—that voice we call our conscience—cries out to us. In complex situations, the voice can be difficult to discern, and we can even learn how to dull that voice into submission, but we cannot really deny that it is there. It is simply the human experience. We can argue about its origins, but it *is* there.

When a person spurns his conscience and fails to do what he knows is right, he subtracts from his character. When he evades his responsibilities, succumbs to temptation, foists his problems and burdens on others, or fails to exert self-discipline, he subtracts from his character. When he attempts to reform the world without reforming himself first, he subtracts from his character.

A person's character is nothing more and nothing less than the sum of his choices. You can't choose your height or race or many other physical traits, but you fine tune your character every time you decide right from wrong and what you personally are going to do about it. Your character is further defined by how you choose to interact with others and the standards of speech and conduct you practice. Character is often listed as a key leadership quality. I actually think character and leadership are one and the same. If you've got character, others will look upon you as a leader—not in the sense that they are eager

to be subservient to you but in the sense that you are someone they admire and freely desire to emulate.

Ravaged by conflict, corruption and tyranny, the world is starving for people of character. Indeed, as much as anything, it is on this matter that the fate of individual liberty has always depended. A free society flourishes when people seek to be models of honor, honesty, and propriety at whatever the cost in material wealth, social status, or popularity. It descends into barbarism when they abandon what's right in favor of self-gratification at the expense of others; when lying, cheating, or stealing are winked at instead of shunned. If you want to be free, if you want to live in a free society, you must assign top priority to raising the caliber of your character and learning from those who already have it in spades. *If you do not govern yourself, you will be governed.*

Character means that there are no matters too small to handle the right way. It's been said that your character is defined by what you do when no one is looking. Cutting corners because "it won't matter much" or "no one will notice" still knocks your character down a notch and can easily become a slippery slope. "Unless you are faithful in small matters," we learn in Luke 16:10, "you will not be faithful in large ones." That's a message that shows up in the teachings of many faiths. Even those of no faith should see the wisdom of it.

Chief among the elements that define strong character are these: honesty, humility, patience, responsibility, self-discipline, self-reliance, optimism, courage, a long-term focus, and a lust for learning. Who in his right mind would want to live in a world without these things?

Dishonest people will lie and cheat and become even bigger liars and cheaters in elected office. People who lack humility become arrogant, condescending, know-it-all central-planner types. Irresponsible citizens blame others for the consequences of their own poor judgment. People who will not discipline themselves invite the intrusive control of others. Those who eschew self-reliance are easily manipulated by those on whom they are dependent. Pessimists dismiss what individuals can accomplish when given the freedom to try. Timid people will allow their rights to be trampled. Myopic citizens will mortgage their future for the sake of a short-term "solution." Closed-minded, head-in-the-sand types don't learn from the lessons of history and human action.

Ever since Samuel Smiles wrote his remarkably influential *Self Help* in 1859, hundreds of books in the same vein have appeared in print. Twentieth-century authors like Dale Carnegie (*How to Win Friends and Influence People*) and John Maxwell (*The 21 Indispensable Qualities of a Leader: Becoming the Person Others Will Want to Follow*) and Stephen Covey (*The Seven Habits of Highly Effective People*) sold millions of copies of their works, all aimed at inspiring people to improve their attitudes or work habits or personal character. So obviously there's been a lot of interest for a long time in at least reading about self-improvement, even if we don't actually do it.

The Importance of Gratitude

An often-overlooked but remarkably important character trait is *gratitude*. I recently picked up a cheap secondhand copy of a 2008 paperback by Dr. Robert A. Emmons entitled *Thanks! How Practicing Gratitude Can Make You Happier*. Emmons is a professor at the University of California and editor-in-chief of the *Journal of Positive Psychology*. At first, I thought I'd skim a few pages, glean a few quot-able quotes and then stick it on the shelf with all the other self-improvement books gathering dust in my basement. But this one grabbed my attention on the first page. I couldn't put it down until I read the other 208.

This isn't just a feel-good collection of generalities and catchy phrases. It's rooted in what the latest sci-ence can teach us. In language a lay reader can easily understand, Emmons reveals groundbreaking re-search into the previously under-examined emotion we call "gratitude." As defined by Emmons, gratitude is the acknowledgement of goodness in one's life and the recognition that the source of this goodness lies at least partially outside one's self.

Years of study by Emmons and his associates show that "grateful people experience higher levels of positive emotions such as joy, enthusiasm, love, happiness, and optimism, and that the practice of gratitude as a discipline protects a person from the destructive impulses of envy, resentment, greed, and bitterness."

A grateful attitude enriches life. Emmons believes it elevates, energizes, inspires, and transforms. The science of it proves that gratitude is an indispensable key to happiness (the more of it you can muster, the happier you'll be), and happiness adds up to nine years to life expectancy. Think about it: haven't you noticed that people of lousy character are rarely grateful for anything?

Gratitude isn't just a knee-jerk, unthinking "thank you." It's much more than a warm and fuzzy sentiment. It's not automatic. Some people, in fact, feel and express it all too rarely. And as grateful a person as you may think you are, chances are you can develop an even more grateful attitude, a task that carries ample rewards that more than compensate for its moral and intellectual challenges.

Emmons cites plenty of evidence for his thesis but most readers will find his seventh and final chapter, a mere twenty-four pages, the most useful part of the book. There the author lays out ten steps (exercises, in fact) for cultivating this critically important emotion. If I had space to tell you here what those steps were, you might not read the book. So if you want a serious self-improvement book, pick this one up. I guarantee that you'll be grateful for the recommendation.

I firmly believe that good example is the best teaching device. That's a view I share with my friend Mark Hyatt, whose influential Character and Education Project is working with schools to help make this very point. We tend to learn and remember stories, especially stories of real people. So to impress the importance of character upon you, I want to tell you about a few more exemplars of it.

Here's one from the 2005 movie "Cinderella Man." The film is a masterpiece from start to finish, but I especially loved an early scene in which boxer James Braddock (played by Russell Crowe) learns that his young son has stolen a sausage. The family is hungry and destitute at the bottom of the Great Depression. The boy was fearful that, like one of his friends whose parents couldn't provide enough to eat, he would be sent to live with relatives who could afford the expense. Braddock does not hesitate on the matter for a second. He immediately escorts the boy to the store to return the sausage and apologize to the butcher. He then lectures his son:

"There's a lot of people worse off than we are. And just because things ain't easy, that don't give you the excuse to take what's not yours, does it? That's stealing, right? We don't steal. No matter what happens, we don't steal. Not ever. You got me?"

His son replies, "Yes," but Braddock presses the point, two more times: "Are you giving me your word?"

"Yes."

"Come on."

"I promise."

Braddock's character ascends to new heights later in the film when he does what no welfare recipient is ever asked to do and what perhaps not one in a million has ever done: he pays the taxpayers back. Now that is character! And he certainly knew how to encourage those qualities in his son—both by his words and by his example.

Hollywood turns out so little these days that inspires character but in 2005 it did produce another movie that I rank among the very best of all time. It's "The Greatest Game Ever Played," the true story of the son of an immigrant, Francis Ouimet, who won the 1913 U.S. Open Golf Championship at the age of twenty. Buy it, or rent it, and watch it as a study in character. Both the main figure, Francis, and the story's secondary hero, Harry Vardon, ooze character from every pore. The traits they so magnificently exhibit include professionalism, perseverance, integrity, sportsmanship, loyalty, and honor. You watch that movie and you'll come away with boundless admiration for Francis and Harry and it's not so much for their great golf abilities as it is because of their sterling characters.

In history, the men and women we most admire and best remember are those whose character stands out because they lived it twenty-four hours every day and did not compromise it. They are not like that fictional character played by the great comedian Groucho Marx, who said, "Those are my principles! If you don't like them, well, *I have others.*"

Changing the Conscience of a Nation

Consider William Wilberforce, the man from Yorkshire who more than any other single individual was responsible for ending slavery throughout the British Empire. His story was recently told in a wonderful biography by Eric Metaxas called "Amazing Grace" and in a beautiful 2006 film by the same title (I highly recommend them both).

Born in 1759, Wilberforce never had the physical presence one would hope to possess in a fight. Boswell called him a "shrimp." Thin and short, Wilberforce compensated with a powerful vision, an appealing eloquence, and an indomitable will.

Elected to Parliament in 1780 at the age of twenty-one, Wilberforce spoke out against the war with America in no uncertain terms, labeling it "cruel, bloody, and impractical." But he drifted from issue to issue without a central focus until a conversion to Christianity sparked what would be a lifelong calling. Revolted by the hideous barbarity of the slave trade then prevalent in the world, he determined in October 1787 to work for its abolition.

Abolitionism was a tall order in the late 1700s. Viewed widely at the time as integral to British naval and commercial success, slavery was big business. It enjoyed broad political support, as well as widespread (though essentially racist) intellectual justification. For seventy-five years before Wilberforce set about to end the trade in slaves, and ultimately slavery itself, Britain enjoyed the sole right by treaty to supply

Spanish colonies with captured Africans. The trade was lucrative for British slavers but savagely merciless for its millions of victims.

Wilberforce labored relentlessly for his cause, forming and assisting organizations to spread the word about the inhumanity of one man owning another. "Our motto must continue to be perseverance," he once told followers. And what a model of perseverance he was! He endured and overcame just about every obstacle imaginable, including ill health, derision from his colleagues, and defeats almost too numerous to count. In any respect, he maintained the highest standard of character, a fact which itself served as a powerful magnet for his cause.

He rose in the House of Commons to give his first abolition speech in 1789, not knowing that it would take another eighteen years before the slave trade would be ended by law. Every year he would introduce an abolition measure, and every year it would go nowhere. At least once, some of his own allies deserted him because the opposition gave them free tickets to attend the theatre during a crucial vote. The war with France that began in the 1790s often put the slavery issue on the back burner. A bloody slave rebellion in the Caribbean seemed to give ammunition to the other side. Wilberforce was often ridiculed and condemned as a traitorous rabble-rouser. He had reason to fear for his life.

Once, in 1805 after yet another defeat in Parliament, Wilberforce was advised by a clerk of the Commons to give up the fight. He replied with the

air of undying optimism that had come to character-
ize his stance on the issue: "I do expect to carry it."

Indeed, what seemed once to be an impossible
dream became reality in 1807. Abolition of the slave
trade won Parliament's overwhelming approval.
Biographer David J. Vaughan reports that "as the
attorney general, Sir Samuel Romilly, stood and
praised the perseverance of Wilberforce, the House
rose to its feet and broke out in cheers. Wilberforce
was so overcome with emotion that he sat head
in hand, tears streaming down his face." Boswell's
shrimp had become a whale.

The trade in slaves was officially over, but ending
slavery itself remained the ultimate prize. To bring
it about, Wilberforce worked for another twenty-six
years, even after he left behind nearly a quarter-
century of service in Parliament in 1825. The great
day finally came on July 26, 1833, when Britain en-
acted a peaceful emancipation (with compensation
to slaveholders) and became the world's first major
nation to unshackle an entire race within its juris-
diction. Hailed as the hero who made it possible,
Wilberforce died three days later. He and his allies
had changed the conscience of a nation.

The lessons of Wilberforce's life reduce to this: a
worthy goal should always inspire. Don't let any set-
back slow you up. Maintain an optimism worthy of
the goal itself, and do all within your character and
power to rally others to the cause.

**Anne Frank may well be the most famous
15-year-old author of the twentieth century. She**

penned but one volume, a diary, while hiding from the Nazis during the German occupation of the Netherlands. "How wonderful it is," she wrote, "that nobody need wait a single moment before starting to improve the world."

Imagine it. Living each day for two years crammed in the hidden rooms of an office building, knowing that at any moment you might be found and hauled off to near-certain death at a concentration camp. Barely a teenager, she managed to write those and many other words of remarkable inspiration before she and her family were discovered in August 1944. They were sent to the Bergen-Belsen camp where Anne died in March 1945, just three months before her sixteenth birthday.

How is it possible for a youngster to see so much light in a dark world, to find within her so much hope and optimism amidst horror? What insight! What power! What character! That's been the magic of Anne Frank for the past seven decades.

Anne Frank's message will be remembered for many more decades to come, hopefully forever. It reminds us that no matter the circumstances, we can make a difference. Our attitude (which itself is largely a function of our character) determines our altitude. If you want to make a better world, start by making a better self; it's the one thing you have considerable control over in almost any situation.

Character Saves Lives

From that same era comes the story of Nicholas Winton. At this writing (Spring 2013), he is still alive and well at 104. He's a personal friend who lives just outside of London.

Winton was a young London stockbroker as war clouds gathered across Europe in 1938-39. A friend convinced him to forgo a Christmas vacation in Switzerland and come to Czechoslovakia instead. Near Prague in December 1938 he was shocked to see Jewish refugees freezing in make-shift camps. Most had been driven from their homes by Nazi occupation of the Sudetenland, the part of Czechoslovakia handed over to Hitler at Munich the previous September.

Winton could have resumed his Swiss vacation, stepping back into the comfortable life he left behind. What could a lone foreigner do to assist so many trapped families? Despite the talk of "peace in our time," Winton knew that Europe was sliding toward war and time was running out for these desperate people. The next steps he took ultimately saved 669 children from death in Nazi camps.

The parents were anxious to get their children to safety, even though it would mean sending them off alone. Getting the children to a country that would accept them seemed an impossible challenge. Nicholas Winton didn't waste a minute. He wrote to governments around the world, pleading for an open door, only to be rejected by every one but two:

Sweden and his own Great Britain. He assembled a small group of volunteers to assist with the effort. Even his mother pitched in.

With five thousand children on his list, Winton searched for foster homes across Britain. British newspapers published his advertisements to highlight the urgent need for foster parents. When enough homes could be found for a group of children, he submitted the necessary paperwork to the Home Office and assisted his team of volunteers in organizing the rail and ship transportation needed to get the children to Britain. He took the lead in raising the funds to pay for the operation.

The first twenty of "Winton's children" left Prague on March 14, 1939. Hitler's troops devoured all of Czechoslovakia the very next day, but Winton's team kept working, sometimes forging documents to slip the children past the Germans. By the time World War II broke out on September 1 the rescue effort had taken 669 children out of the country in eight separate groups by rail. The last batch of 250 would have been the largest of all, but war prompted the Nazis to stop all departures. Sadly, none of those children lived to see the Allied victory less than six years later. Pitifully few of the parents did either.

Why did Nicholas Winton take on a challenge ignored by almost everyone else? I asked him that very question at his home in Maidenhead, England, in 2006. "Because it was the thing to do and I thought I could help," he told us. Today, the "Winton children" plus their children and grandchildren number about six thousand people.

Winton's example illustrates that character not only enriches lives, it *saves* lives too.

George Washington was one of our best presidents because he knew at every moment that maintaining the highest standards in every aspect of life, public and private, was critical to placing the new nation on the right path. A man of lesser character might not have carried us through such a critical period, or would have put us on a different and more perilous path. He drew the stunned admiration of the world when he passed up the opportunity to seize power for himself and placed his trust instead in a free and virtuous people.

Washington understood the link between character and liberty. Listen to him speaking to the nation in his Farewell Address of 1796:

It is substantially true that virtue and morality is a necessary spring of popular government. The rule, indeed, extends with more or less force to every species of free government. Who that is a sincere friend to it can look with indifference upon attempts to shake the foundation of the fabric?

Washington was hardly alone on this matter. Another giant of liberty in that day, James Madison, wrote in 1788 that "To suppose that any form of government will secure liberty or happiness without any virtue in the people, is a chimerical idea."

Untying the Gordian Knot

Thomas Jefferson's words of wisdom on this issue of character are well worth your serious attention:

> Give up money, give up fame, give up science, give up the earth itself and all it contains, rather than do an immoral act. And never suppose, that in any possible situation, or under any circumstances, it is best for you to do a dishonorable thing, however slightly so it may appear to you. Whenever you are to do a thing, though it can never be known but to yourself, ask yourself how you would act were all the world looking at you, and act accordingly.
>
> Encourage all your virtuous dispositions, and exercise them whenever an opportunity arises; being assured that they will gain strength by exercise, as a limb of the body does, and that exercise will make them habitual. From the practice of the purest virtue, you may be assured you will derive the most sublime comforts in every moment of life, and in the moment of death. If ever you find yourself environed with difficulties and perplexing circumstances, out of which you are at a loss how to extricate yourself, do what is right, and be assured that that will extricate you the best out of the worst situations.

Though you cannot see, when you take one step, what will be the next, yet follow truth, justice, and plain dealing, and never fear their leading you out of the labyrinth, in the easiest manner possible. The knot which you thought a Gordian one, will un-tie itself before you. Nothing is so mistaken as the supposition that a person is to extricate himself from a difficulty, by intrigue, by chicanery, by dissimulation, by trimming, by an untruth, by an injustice. This increases the difficulties tenfold; and those who pursue these methods, get themselves so involved at length, that they can turn no way but their infamy becomes more exposed.

What those Founders were getting at is the notion that liberty is built upon the ability of a society to govern itself, without government intervention. This ability to self-govern is itself built upon—you guessed it—*individual character*.

Here's a name you may not have heard of: Fanny Crosby. Fanny Crosby holds the record for having written more hymns than any other human being—at least eight thousand—including the popular "Blessed Assurance." She died in 1915 at the age of ninety-five. She was the first woman in our history to address the United States Congress. She personally met or knew every president of the United States from John Quincy Adams to Woodrow Wilson, maybe more than any other single person in our country's history, alive or dead. And guess what?

She never in her ninety-five years had any recollection of ever having *seen* a thing. She was blind from the age of six months, the result of a botched treatment for an eye infection. She spoke frequently and in many places of how important it was for a person's character to shine so it could overcome any and all handicaps and obstacles. Many who knew her regarded her as a saint of enormous inspiration.

By citing many people from the past, I certainly don't mean to suggest there aren't heroes of character in our own time. Indeed, they are all around us, though I sometimes fear their numbers are dwindling. Today's heroes of character include teachers who teach truth and defy political correctness; businessmen and businesswomen who build their enterprises without seeking special favors from political friends; parents who spend time with their children and raise them properly in a world with endless negative influences; and really, *anyone* who tries to live his or her life in ways that don't compromise integrity.

Over four decades I've written scores of articles, essays, and columns on economics; taught the subject at the university level; and given hundreds of speeches on it. In recent years the nexus between the economics of a free society and individual character has worked its way into my writing, speaking, and thinking with increasing emphasis. I now believe that nexus is the central issue we must address if our liberties and free economy are to be restored and preserved.

Scholars and writers who believe in a free society have stressed the need for sound public-policy research and basic economic education. In the past thirty years or so, think tanks and new media have sprung up like mushrooms to provide both. Though important, they are proving to be insufficient to overcome trends that are eroding our liberties. Why?

The Missing Ingredient

To some extent, policy research (though I fully support it) is essentially locking the barn door after the horse has left. It targets politicians and media commentators at stages in their lives when they are largely set in their ways and interested more in personal advancement than truth and liberty.

Economic education is certainly needed because young minds are not typically getting it in schools. But even if economic education were dramatically improved, a free society wouldn't necessarily follow. Just like public-policy research, it can be undone by harmful themes in popular culture (movies, religion, music, literature, and even sports) and in the standards of conduct people practice as adults.

Even among the most ardent supporters of a free society are people who "leak" when it comes to their own bottom lines. A recent example was the corn farmer who berated me for opposing ethanol subsidies. Does he not understand basic economics? I've known him for years, and I believe he does. But that understanding melted away with the corrupting lure of a handout. His extensive economics knowledge was not enough to keep him from the public trough. We are losing the sense of shame that once accompanied the act of theft, private or public.

The missing ingredient here is character. In America's first century, we possessed it in abundance and even though there were no think tanks, very little economic education, and even less policy research, it kept our liberties substantially intact. People generally opposed the expansion of government power not because they read policy studies or earned degrees in economics, but because they placed a high priority on character. Using government to get something at somebody else's expense, or mortgaging the future for near-term gain, seemed dishonest and cynical to them, if not downright sinful and immoral.

One of the strongest arguments for liberty, in my mind, is the fact that it is the one and only social/political/economic arrangement that *demands* high character. No other man-designed or centrally planned concoction does. For a people to be free, they must seek to live by the highest standards of character.

Within government, character is what differentiates a politician from a statesman. Statesmen don't seek public office for personal gain or attention. They often are people who take time out from productive careers to temporarily serve the public. They don't have to work for government because that's all they know how to do. They stand for a principled vision, not for what they think citizens will fall for. When a statesman gets elected, he doesn't forget the public-spirited citizens who sent him to office, becoming a mouthpiece for the permanent bureaucracy or some special interest that greased his campaign.

Because they seek the truth, statesmen are more likely to do what's right than what may be politically popular at the moment. You know where they stand because they say what they mean and they mean what they say. They do not engage in class warfare, race-baiting, or other divisive or partisan tactics that pull people apart. They do not buy votes with tax dollars. They don't make promises they can't keep or intend to break. They take responsibility for their actions. A statesman doesn't try to pull himself up by dragging somebody else down, and he doesn't try to convince people they're victims just so he can posture as their savior.

Unthinkably Bad Policies

When it comes to managing public finances, states-men prioritize. They don't behave as though government deserves an endlessly larger share of other people's money. They exhibit the courage to cut less important expenses to make way for more pressing ones. They don't try to build empires. Instead, they keep government within its proper bounds and trust in what free and enterprising people can accomplish. Politicians think that they're smart enough to plan other people's lives; statesmen are wise enough to understand what utter folly such arrogant attitudes really are. Statesmen, in other words, possess a level of character that an ordinary politician does not.

We've heard a lot of talk lately about certain companies being "too big to fail." But in dealing with this supposed problem, we've handed huge chunks of our lives and economy over to a government that is arguably too big to succeed. We've put the country on the road to financial insolvency. People of character don't do that. To a genuine statesman, such policies would be unthinkable.

By almost any measure, the standards we as citizens keep and expect of those we elect have slipped badly in recent years. Though everybody complains about politicians who pander, perhaps they do it because we are increasingly a pander-able people. Too many are willing to look the other way when politicians misbehave, as long as they are of the right party or deliver the goods we personally want.

Our celebrity-drenched culture focuses incessantly on the vapid and the irresponsible. Our role models would make our grandparents cringe. To many, insisting on sterling character seems too straight-laced and old-fashioned. We cut corners and sacrifice character all the time for power, money, attention, or other ephemeral gratifications.

Bad character leads to bad policy and bad economics, which is bad for liberty. Ultimately, whether we live free and in harmony with the laws of nature or stumble in the dark thrall of dependency and tyranny is less a political

or economic issue than it is a *character* issue. Without character, a free society is not just unlikely, it's impossible.

In June 2003, my best friend and business colleague Joe Overton was killed in a plane crash at the age of forty-three. He taught me more about the importance of character than anyone else I have ever known. He could teach it because he lived it. While composing a eulogy for his funeral, I came across a few lines about what the world needs. I've never learned who the author was so I can't offer appropriate credit, and in any event, I added a lot to it. It not only describes what the world desperately needs, it described my friend Joe perfectly. I share it with you as I close:

The world needs more men and women who do not have a price at which they can be bought; who do not borrow from integrity to pay for expediency; who have their priorities straight and in proper order; whose handshake is an ironclad contract; who are not afraid of taking risks to advance what is right; and who are as honest in small matters as they are in large ones.

The world needs more men and women whose ambitions are big enough to include others; who know how to win with grace and lose with dignity; who do not believe that shrewdness and cunning and ruthlessness are the three keys to success; who still have friends they made twenty years ago; who put principle and consistency above politics or

*personal advancement; and who are not afraid
to go against the grain of popular opinion.*

*The world needs more men and women who
do not forsake what is right just to get consensus
because it makes them look good; who know how
important it is to lead by example, not by barking
orders; who would not have you do something
they would not do themselves; who work to turn
even the most adverse circumstances into oppor-
tunities to learn and improve; who respect the
lives, property, and rights of their fellow men and
women; and who love even those who have done
some injustice or unfairness to them.*

*The world, in other words, needs more men and
women of character.*

Make this day the start of a lifelong commitment
to building character. Be the kind of virtuous example that others will respect, admire, emulate,
and remember. Ask yourself every day, "Am I good
enough for liberty?" and if you come up short, work
on it. You'll not only go to your reward some day
with a smile and a clear conscience, you will enhance
many other lives along the way. How can any of us
settle for any less?

Introduction: The Character Message of "I, Pencil"

More than half a century ago (December 1958, to be precise), the Foundation for Economic Education (FEE) published for the first time an essay with a humble title, "I, Pencil." The author was Leonard E. Read, FEE's founder, and before he died in 1983 he realized he had penned a classic. Many first-time readers of it never see the world quite the same again. Its message? *No one person—repeat, no one, no matter how smart or how many degrees follow his name—could create from scratch, entirely by himself, a small, everyday pencil, let alone a car or an airplane.*

"I, Pencil" is more than an ingenious explanation of the wondrous, even *miraculous*, workings of a free market. We include it here as part of this book about character because it speaks volumes about one of the most important character traits a free society requires—humility.

Think about it: a mere pencil—a simple thing, yet beyond any one person's complete comprehension. Think what went into it: the mining of zinc, graphite, and copper; the logging of cedar or other wood, and all the technology involved in the saws, trucks, rope, and railroads that took it from the forest to the factory; the castor beans that became an ingredient in the lacquer; the dozens of chemicals found or produced and then distilled into the pencil's parts, from the eraser to the glue that holds it all together. Countless people and skills assemble miraculously in the marketplace without a single mastermind, indeed, without anyone who knows more than a corner of the whole process.

It is a message that humbles the high and mighty. It pricks the inflated egos of those who think they know how to mind everybody else's business. It explains in plain language why central planning of a society or an economy is an exercise in arrogance and futility, or what Nobel Prize-winning economist F. A. Hayek termed "a pretense to knowledge." If I can't make a pencil, I'd better be careful about how smart I think I am.

Maximilian Robespierre blessed the horrific French Revolution with this chilling declaration, "On ne saurait faire une omelette sans casser des oeufs." Translation: "One can't expect to make an omelet without breaking eggs." He labored tirelessly to plan the lives of others and became the architect of the Revolution's bloodiest phase—the Reign of Terror. Robespierre and his guillotine broke eggs by the thousands in a vain effort to impose a utopian society with government planners at the top and everybody else at the bottom.

That French experience is one example in a disturbingly familiar pattern. Call them what you will—socialist, interventionist, collectivist, statist—history is littered with their presumptuous plans for rearranging society to fit their vision of the common good, plans that always fail as they kill or impoverish people in the process. If big government ever earns a final epitaph, it will be this: "Here lies a contrivance engineered by know-it-alls who broke eggs with abandon but never, *ever* created an omelet."

None of the Robespierres of the world knew how to make a pencil, yet they wanted to make entire societies. How utterly preposterous, and mournfully tragic! The Robespierres, the Hitlers, and the Stalins of the world didn't suffer from low self-esteem.

Liberty requires men and women of character who know their limitations, who are humble enough to realize they can't possibly plan the lives and economy of hundreds of millions of people. Socialism and central planning are the delusions of ego-maniacs and are no part of the vision of people of introspection and character.

We will miss a large implication of Leonard Read's message if we assume it aims only at the tyrants whose names we all know. The lesson of "I, Pencil" is not that error begins when the planners plan big. It begins the moment one tosses humility aside, assumes he knows the unknowable, and employs the force of government to control more and more of other people's lives. That's not just a national disease. It can be very local indeed.

In our midst are people who think that if only they had government power on their side, they could pick tomorrow's winners and losers in the marketplace, set prices or rents where they ought to be, decide which forms of energy should power our homes and cars, and choose which industries should survive and which should die. They make grandiose promises they can't possibly keep without bankrupting all of us. They should stop for a few moments and learn a little humility from a lowly writing implement.

Now, please enjoy Leonard E. Read's remarkable "I, Pencil."

I, Pencil

By Leonard E. Read

I am a lead pencil—the ordinary wooden pencil familiar to all boys and girls and adults who can read and write.

Writing is both my vocation and my avocation; that's all I do.

You may wonder why I should write a genealogy. Well, to begin with, my story is interesting. And, next, I am a mystery—more so than a tree or a sunset or even a flash of lightning. But, sadly, I am taken for granted by those who use me, as if I were a mere incident and without background. This supercilious attitude relegates me to the level of the commonplace. This is a species of the grievous error in which mankind cannot too long persist without peril. For, the wise G. K. Chesterton observed, "We are perishing for want of wonder, not for want of wonders."

I, Pencil, simple though I appear to be, merit your wonder and awe, a claim I shall attempt to prove. In fact, if you can understand me—no, that's too much to ask of anyone—if you can become aware of the miraculousness which I symbolize, you can help save the freedom mankind is so unhappily losing. I have a profound lesson to teach. And I can teach this lesson better than can an automobile or an airplane

39

or a mechanical dishwasher because—well, because I am seemingly so simple.

Simple? Yet, not a single person on the face of this earth knows how to make me. This sounds fantastic, doesn't it? Especially when it is realized that there are about one and one-half billion of my kind produced in the United States each year.

Pick me up and look me over. What do you see? Not much meets the eye—there's some wood, lacquer, the printed labeling, graphite lead, a bit of metal, and an eraser.

Innumerable Antecedents

Just as you cannot trace your family tree back very far, so is it impossible for me to name and explain all my antecedents. But I would like to suggest enough of them to impress upon you the richness and complexity of my background.

My family tree begins with what in fact is a tree, a cedar of straight grain that grows in northern California and Oregon. Now contemplate all the saws and trucks and rope and the countless other gear used in harvesting and carting the cedar logs to the railroad siding. Think of all the persons and the numberless skills that went into their fabrication: the mining of ore, the making of steel and its refinement into saws, axes, motors; the growing of hemp and bringing it through all the stages to heavy and strong rope; the logging camps with their beds and mess halls, the cookery and the raising of all the foods. Why, untold thousands of persons had a hand in every cup of coffee the loggers drink!

The logs are shipped to a mill in San Leandro, California. Can you imagine the individuals who make flat cars and rails and railroad engines and who construct and install the communication systems incidental thereto? These legions are among my antecedents.

Consider the millwork in San Leandro. The cedar logs are cut into small, pencil-length slats less than one-fourth of an inch in thickness. These are kiln dried and then tinted for the same reason women put rouge on their faces. People prefer that I look pretty, not a pallid white. The slats are waxed and kiln dried again. How many skills went into the making of the tint and the kilns, into supplying the heat, the light and power, the belts, motors, and all the other things a mill requires? Sweepers in the mill among my ancestors? Yes, and included are the men who poured the concrete for the dam of a Pacific Gas & Electric Company hydroplant which supplies the mill's power!

Don't overlook the ancestors present and distant who have a hand in transporting sixty carloads of slats across the nation.

Once in the pencil factory—$4,000,000 in machinery and building, all capital accumulated by thrifty and saving parents of mine—each slat is given eight grooves by a complex machine, after which another machine lays leads in every other slat, applies glue, and places another slat atop—a lead sandwich, so to speak. Seven brothers and I are mechanically carved from this "wood-clinched" sandwich.

My "lead" itself—it contains no lead at all—is complex. The graphite is mined in Ceylon [Sri Lanka]. Consider these miners and those who make their many tools and the makers of the paper sacks in which the graphite is shipped and those who make the string that ties the sacks and those who put them aboard ships and those who make the ships. Even the lighthouse keepers along the way assisted in my birth—and the harbor pilots.

The graphite is mixed with clay from Mississippi in which ammonium hydroxide is used in the refining process. Then wetting agents are added such as sulfonated tallow—animal fats chemically reacted with sulfuric acid. After passing through numerous machines, the mixture finally appears as endless extrusions—as from a sausage grinder—cut to size, dried, and baked for several hours at 1,850 degrees Fahrenheit. To increase their strength and smoothness the leads are then treated with a hot mixture which includes candelilla wax from Mexico, paraffin wax, and hydrogenated natural fats.

My cedar receives six coats of lacquer. Do you know all the ingredients of lacquer? Who would think that the growers of castor beans and the refiners of castor oil are a part of it? They are. Why, even the processes by which the lacquer is made a beautiful yellow involve the skills of more persons than one can enumerate!

Observe the labeling. That's a film formed by applying heat to carbon black mixed with resins. How do you make resins and what, pray, is carbon black?

My bit of metal—the ferrule—is brass. Think of all the persons who mine zinc and copper and those who have the skills to make shiny sheet brass from these products of nature. Those black rings on my ferrule are black nickel. What is black nickel and how is it applied? The complete story of why the center of my ferrule has no black nickel on it would take pages to explain.

Then there's my crowning glory, inelegantly referred to in the trade as "the plug," the part man uses to erase the errors he makes with me. An ingredient called "factice" is what does the erasing. It is a rubber-like product made by reacting rapeseed oil from the Dutch East Indies [Indonesia] with sulfur chloride. Rubber, contrary to the common notion, is only for binding purposes. Then, too, there are numerous vulcanizing and accelerating agents. The pumice comes from Italy; and the pigment which gives "the plug" its color is cadmium sulfide.

No One Knows

Does anyone wish to challenge my earlier assertion that no single person on the face of this earth knows how to make me?

Actually, millions of human beings have had a hand in my creation, no one of whom even knows more than a very few of the others. Now, you may say that I go too far in relating the picker of a coffee berry in far-off Brazil and food growers elsewhere to my creation; that this is an extreme position. I shall stand by my claim. There isn't a single person in all these millions, including the president of the pencil company, who contributes more than a tiny, infinitesimal bit of know-how. From the standpoint of know-how the only difference between the miner of graphite in Ceylon and the logger in Oregon is in the type of know-how. Neither the miner nor the logger can be dispensed with, any more than can the chemist at the factory or the worker in the oil field— paraffin being a by-product of petroleum.

Here is an astounding fact: Neither the worker in the oil field nor the chemist nor the digger of graphite or clay nor any who mans or makes the ships or trains or trucks nor the one who runs the machine that does the knurling on my bit of metal nor the president of the company performs his singular task because he wants me. Each one wants me less, perhaps, than does a child in the first grade. Indeed, there are some among this vast multitude who never saw a pencil nor would they know how to use one. Their motivation is other than me. Perhaps it is something like this: Each of these millions sees that he can thus exchange his tiny know-how for the goods and services he needs or wants. I may or may not be among these items.

No Master Mind
There is a fact still more astounding: the absence of a master mind, of anyone dictating or forcibly

directing these countless actions which bring me into being. No trace of such a person can be found. Instead, we find the "Invisible Hand" at work. This is the mystery to which I earlier referred.

It has been said that "only God can make a tree." Why do we agree with this? Isn't it because we realize that we ourselves could not make one? Indeed, can we even describe a tree? We cannot, except in superficial terms. We can say, for instance, that a certain molecular configuration manifests itself as a tree. But what mind is there among men that could even record, let alone direct, the constant changes in molecules that transpire in the life span of a tree? Such a feat is utterly unthinkable!

I, Pencil, am a complex combination of miracles: a tree, zinc, copper, graphite, and so on. But to these miracles which manifest themselves in nature an even more extraordinary miracle has been added: the configuration of creative human energies—millions of tiny know-hows configurating naturally and spontaneously in response to human necessity and desire and in the absence of any human masterminding! Since only God can make a tree, I insist that only God could make me. Man can no more direct these millions of know-hows to bring me into being than he can put molecules together to create a tree.

The above is what I meant when writing, "If you can become aware of the miraculousness which I symbolize, you can help save the freedom mankind is so unhappily losing." For, if one is aware that these know-hows will naturally, yes, automatically, arrange themselves into creative and productive patterns in response to human necessity and demand—that is, in the absence of governmental or any other coercive master-minding—then one will possess an absolutely essential ingredient for freedom: a faith in free people. Freedom is impossible without this faith.

Once government has had a monopoly of a creative activity such, for instance, as the delivery of the mails, most individuals will believe that the mail could not be efficiently delivered by men acting freely. And here is the reason: Each one acknowledges that he himself doesn't know how to do all the things incident to mail delivery. He also recognizes that no other individual could do it. These assumptions are correct. No individual possesses enough know-how to perform a nation's mail delivery any more than any individual possesses enough know-how to make a pencil. Now, in the absence of faith in free people—in the unawareness that millions of tiny know-hows would naturally and miraculously form and cooperate to satisfy this necessity—the individual cannot help but reach the erroneous conclusion that mail can be delivered only by governmental "masterminding."

Testimony Galore

If I, Pencil, were the only item that could offer testimony on what men and women can accomplish when free to try, then those with little faith would have a fair case. However, there is testimony galore;

it's all about us and on every hand. Mail delivery is exceedingly simple when compared, for instance, to the making of an automobile or a calculating machine or a grain combine or a milling machine or to tens of thousands of other things. Delivery? Why, in this area where men have been left free to try, they deliver the human voice around the world in less than one second; they deliver an event visually and in motion to any person's home when it is happening; they deliver 150 passengers from Seattle to Baltimore in less than four hours; they deliver gas from Texas to one's range or furnace in New York at unbelievably low rates and without subsidy; they deliver each four pounds of oil from the Persian Gulf to our Eastern Seaboard—halfway around the world—for less money than the government charges for delivering a one-ounce letter across the street!

The lesson I have to teach is this: Leave all creative energies uninhibited. Merely organize society to act in harmony with this lesson. Let society's legal apparatus remove all obstacles the best it can. Permit these creative know-hows freely to flow. Have faith that free men and women will respond to the Invisible Hand. This faith will be confirmed. I, Pencil, seemingly simple though I am, offer the miracle of my creation as testimony that this is a practical faith, as practical as the sun, the rain, a cedar tree, the good earth.

Afterword

By Milton Friedman, Nobel Laureate, 1976

Leonard Read's delightful story, "I, Pencil," has become a classic, and deservedly so. I know of no other piece of literature that so succinctly, persuasively, and effectively illustrates the meaning of both Adam Smith's Invisible Hand—the possibility of co-operation without coercion—and Friedrich Hayek's emphasis on the importance of dispersed knowledge and the role of the price system in communicating information that "will make the individuals do the desirable things without anyone having to tell them what to do."

We used Leonard's story in our television show, *Free to Choose*, and in the accompanying book of the same title to illustrate "the power of the market" (the title of both the first segment of the TV show and chapter one of the book). We summarized the story and then went on to say:

> *None of the thousands of persons involved in producing the pencil performed his task because he wanted a pencil. Some among them never saw a pencil and would not know what it is for. Each saw his work as a way to get the goods and services he wanted—goods and services we produced in order to get the pencil we wanted. Every time we*

49

go to the store and buy a pencil, we are exchang-
ing a little bit of our services for the infinitesimal
amount of services that each of the thousands con-
tributed toward producing the pencil.

It is even more astounding that the pencil was
ever produced. No one sitting in a central office
gave orders to these thousands of people. No mili-
tary police enforced the orders that were not given.
These people live in many lands, speak different
languages, practice different religions, may even
hate one another—yet none of these differences
prevented them from cooperating to produce a
pencil. How did it happen? Adam Smith gave us
the answer two hundred years ago.

"I, Pencil" is a typical Leonard Read product:
imaginative, simple yet subtle, breathing the love of
freedom that imbued everything Leonard wrote or
did. As in the rest of his work, he was not trying to
tell people what to do or how to conduct themselves.
He was simply trying to enhance individuals' understanding of themselves and of the system they live in.

That was his basic credo and one that he stuck
to consistently during his long period of service to
the public—not public service in the sense of government service. Whatever the pressure, he stuck
to his guns, refusing to compromise his principles.
That was why he was so effective in keeping alive,
in the early days, and then spreading the basic idea
that human freedom required private property, free
competition, and severely limited government.

RESOURCES AND BACKGROUND

• Business Ethics

"Would You Lie To Get Ahead?"
http://www.cbsnews.com/8301-500395_162-
57472768/would-you-lie-to-get-ahead/

A recent report by corporate governance specialist Labaton Sucharow showed that 24 percent of financial services executives polled by the law firm believed that unethical or illegal conduct might be required for professional success. Moreover, 16 percent said that they would commit a crime if they thought they could get away with it.

"Ethical Warning Looming in U.S. Workplaces"
http://www.marketwatch.com/story/ethical-
warning-looming-in-us-workplaces-2012-01-23

Last year, nearly 8.8 million Americans felt the sting of workplace retaliation—a 33 percent increase in negative payback from the year before. That surge, identified by the Ethics Resource Center in its biennial survey of ethics in the workplace, is an ominous trend that strongly suggests that ethics violations at U.S. companies are about to go up.

- *Among workers who reported misconduct, more than one in five experienced retaliation in return.*
- *A growing number of employees say they feel pressure to compromise standards.*
- *Fewer workers believe senior leadership is committed to ethical conduct. A growing number (40 percent) say their direct supervisors don't display ethical behavior.*
- *Ethics cultures are on decline. At 47 percent, the share of businesses with weak cultures is near an all-time high.*

"Key Findings, 2011 National Business Ethics Survey (NBES)"

http://www.ethics.org/topic/national-surveys

- *Reporting of misconduct is now at near highs.*
- *Retaliation against employee whistleblowers rose sharply.*
- *The percentage of employees who perceived pressure to compromise standards in order to do their jobs climbed five points since 2009 to 13 percent.*
- *The share of companies with weak ethics cultures also climbed to near-record levels.*

"Ethics Study: More Employees Report Seeing Illegal Donations"

http://www.rollcall.com/news/ethics_study_
more_employees_report_seeing_illegal_donations-
211451-1.html?pos=hftxt

The number of employees of major companies who claim to have witnessed illegal contributions to public officials is four times higher than it was two years ago, according to a new study from a business ethics watchdog group.

Four percent of 4,600 private-sector employees surveyed this fall by the Ethics Resource Center said they witnessed improper contributions to campaigns and parties. By comparison, only 1 percent of respondents reported these transgressions in the group's previous study, completed in 2009.

"Whistleblowers Face Most Corporate Retaliation Ever in 2011"

http://articles.latimes.com/2012/jan/06/business/
la-fi-mo-whistleblower-backlash-20120106

More employees than ever before turned whistleblower against unethical behavior last year, but they also suffered the highest amount of backlash in history from their bosses. Nearly half of all workers witnessed some sort of misconduct, according to a report from research group Ethics Resource Center. Of those, 65 percent reported the wrongdoing—a record number. Also at an all-time high: the 22 percent of whistleblowers who said their companies struck back at them for spilling the beans. Companies tend to act differently in uncertain economic times, taking more risks as the business environment improves, according to the ERC.

• Cheating

"75 to 98 Percent of College Students Have Cheated"
http://education-portal.com/articles/75_to_98_Percent_of_College_Students_Have_Cheated.html

Back in 1940, only 20 percent of college students admitted to cheating during their academic careers. Today, that number has increased to a range of 75–98 percent.

"8 Astonishing Stats on Academic Cheating"
http://oedb.org/library/features/8-astonishing-stats-on-academic-cheating

Some 60.8 percent of polled college students admitted to cheating. An admittedly informal 2007 poll conducted by the popular website CollegeHumor.com revealed that 60.8 percent of 30,000 respondents—most of them within its core demographic—confessed to cheating on their assignments and tests. This lines up closely with a questionnaire sent out to Rutgers students as well, to which 68 percent of students confessed that they had broken the university's explicit anti-cheating rules. And the number only seems to swell as the years progress, with freshmen the most likely to fudge their way through class.

The same poll revealed that 16.5 percent of them didn't regret it. Probably the most disconcerting find that the very same CollegeHumor poll unearthed is the fact that 16.5 percent of those who admitted to cheating felt no guilt whatsoever for their breach of ethics. It did not go into any details regarding why, of course, but one wonders if today's culture of entitlement and success without regard to the well-being of others plays a major role in such callous attitudes. With so many scholarships, awards, internships, and other incentives at stake, it's entirely possible that those reporting no regrets considered their actions justified when rewarded for their "success."

• Dependency

"U.S. Government Increases National Debt—and Keeps 128 Million People on Government Programs"
http://www.heritage.org/research/reports/2013/01/us-government-increases-national-debtand-keeps-128-million-people-on-government-programs

Between 1988 and 2011, the amount of the U.S. population that receives assistance from the federal government grew by 62 percent. That means that more than 41 percent of the U.S. population is enrolled in at least one federal assistance program. To make matters worse, per capita expenditures on recipients are rising as well. In 2010, over 70 percent of all federal spending went to dependence-creating programs.

"Government Dependents Outnumber Those with Private Sector Jobs in 11 U.S. States"
www.westernjournalism.com/government-
dependents-outnumber-those-with-private-sector-
jobs-in-11-u-s-states/

In 11 different U.S. states, the number of government dependents exceeds the number of private sector workers. This list of states includes some of the biggest states in the country: California, New York, Illinois, Ohio, Maine, Kentucky, South Carolina, Mississippi, Alabama, New Mexico, and Hawaii.

• Financial Responsibility

"A Third of Public Says It's Sometimes OK for Homeowners to Stop Making Mortgage Payments"
Pew Research Center, 2010,
http://www.pewsocialtrends.org/2010/09/15/
a-third-of-public-says-sometimes-ok-for-
homeowners-to-stop-making-mortgage-payments

A Barometer of Modern Morals
Pew Research Center, 2006
http://www.pewsocialtrends.org/2006/03/28/
a-barometer-of-modern-morals/

Earlier this year the IRS reported that in 2001 (the last year for which it had conducted such research) there was a gross "tax gap" of $345 billion, resulting from an overall non-compliance rate of about 16 percent. Of that gap, the biggest missing slice, some $197 billion, was from underreporting of income on individual income tax returns; most of that missing sum, in turn, resulted from underreporting of business income on those individual returns, the IRS found.

• Literature/Writing

"The Cultural Salience of Moral Character and Virtue Declined in Twentieth Century America"
By Pelin Kesebir and Selin Kesebir, *Journal of Positive Psychology*, 2012
http://www.papsyblog.org/2012/09/the-cultural-salience-of-moral.html

Abstract: In a large corpus of American books, we tracked how frequently words related to moral excellence and virtue appeared over the twentieth century. Considering the well-established cultural trend in the United States toward greater individualism and its implications for the moral domain, we predicted that morality and virtue terms would appear with diminishing frequency in American books. Two studies supported our predictions: Study 1 showed a decline in the use of general moral terms such as virtue, decency, and conscience throughout the twentieth century. In Study 2, we examined the appearance frequency of fifty virtue words (e.g., honesty, patience, compassion) and found a significant decline for 74 percent of them. Overall, our findings suggest that during the twentieth century, moral ideals and virtues have largely waned from the public conversation.

• Public Opinion

"Moral Values in Decline"
http://www.gallup.com/poll/147794/fewer-americans-down-moral-values.aspx

About 7 in 10 Americans (69 percent) now say moral values in the country as a whole are getting worse. Roughly two-thirds—65 percent—now have a negative view of moral values. This represents the percentage of Americans who think moral values are only fair or poor and either worsening or staying the same.

"Most Americans Say Moral Values in Decline"
http://www.huffingtonpost.com/2010/05/17/most-americans-say-moral_n_579408.html

Three-quarters of Americans say the country's moral values are worsening. The number of Americans who say the nation's moral values are in decline grew by 5 percent since last year.

Pollsters also found 45 percent of Americans believe that current moral values are in a poor state. This number is equal to last year's, which was the highest since 2002. Only 15 percent of Americans believe the country's morality is in an excellent or good state.

"Poll: Americans Say Moral Values Getting Worse"
http://www.christianpost.com/news/poll-americans-say-moral-values-getting-worse-22055/#Aed4kygF95xTyFPl.99

Some 81 percent of adults say the nation's "state of moral values" is getting worse, compared to only 11 percent who say values are improving.

"Why Young Americans Can't Think Morally"
http://www.nationalreview.com/articles/277693/why-young-americans-can-t-think-morally-dennis-prager

When asked to describe a moral dilemma they had faced, two-thirds of the young people either couldn't answer the question or described problems that are not moral at all. Moral thinking didn't enter the picture, even when considering things like drunken driving, cheating in school or cheating on a partner.

The default position, which most of them came back to again and again, is that moral choices are just a matter of individual taste.

As one put it, "I mean, I guess what makes something right is how I feel about it. But different people feel different ways, so I couldn't speak on behalf of anyone else as to what's right and wrong."

Morality was once revealed, inherited, and shared, but now it's thought of as something that emerges in the privacy of your own heart.

About the Author

Lawrence W. ("Larry") Reed is president of the Foundation for Economic Education (FEE) in Atlanta, Georgia. He became president of FEE in 2008. Prior to that, he was a founder and president for twenty years of the Mackinac Center for Public Policy in Midland, Michigan. He also taught Economics full time and chaired the Department of Economics at Northwood University in Michigan from 1977 to 1984.

He holds a BA degree in economics from Grove City College (1975) and an MA degree in history from Slippery Rock State University (1978), both in Pennsylvania. He holds two honorary doctorates, one from Central Michigan University (public administration, 1993) and Northwood University (laws, 2008).

A champion for liberty, Reed has authored over one thousand newspaper columns and articles, and dozens of articles in magazines and journals in the United States and abroad. His writings have appeared in *The Wall Street Journal, Christian Science Monitor, USA Today, Baltimore Sun, Detroit News,* and *Detroit Free Press,* among many others. He has authored or co-authored five books, the most recent ones being *A Republic—If We Can Keep It* and *Striking the Root: Essays on Liberty.* He is frequently interviewed on radio talk shows and has appeared as a guest on numerous television programs, including those anchored by Judge Andrew Napolitano and John Stossel on FOX Business News.

Reed has delivered at least seventy-five speeches annually in the past thirty years—in virtually every state and dozens of countries from Bulgaria to China to Bolivia. His best-known lectures include "Seven Principles of Sound Policy" and "Great Myths of the Great Depression"—both of which have been translated into more than a dozen languages and distributed worldwide.

His interests in political and economic affairs have taken him as a freelance journalist to eighty-one countries on six continents. He is a member of the prestigious Mont Pelerin Society and an advisor to numerous organizations around the world. He served for fifteen years as a member of the board (and one term as president) of the State Policy Network. His numerous recognitions include the "Champion of Freedom" award from the Mackinac Center for Public Policy and the "Distinguished Alumni" award from Grove City College.

He is a native of Pennsylvania and a thirty-year resident of Michigan, and now resides in Newnan, Georgia.

INSPIRE

FEE has been and will always be the source for introductory, optimistic, youth-focused free-market education with an emphasis on the Austrian School's perspective in economics. We also hope to inspire our students. We aim for the "aha!" moment, when the education and fellowship offered by FEE connects the newcomer to the freedom philosophy and its community. This connection will touch off a lifetime of engagement as each student becomes a leader for liberty, inspiring the next generation in turn.

EDUCATE

For 50 years now, FEE has been famous for its summer seminars, bringing students from across the globe to FEE for week long, in-depth discussions of Austrian Economics, Current Events, History and other topics. An exciting introduction to the world of classical liberal traditions and free-market education is what turns FEE's students into life-long lovers of liberty and future leaders for a freer world.

CONNECT

When FEE was established in 1946, it was the only free-market institution in America. It did everything to keep the flame of liberty alight through some very dark times. The freedom movement is now diverse, strong and numerous with institutions and think-tanks in every state and across the globe. In light of this change, FEE works with other organizations, leveraging our capabilities and providing a pathway for our alumni to grow and find their niche in the liberty movement. Community is important to FEE and to our students.

GIVE TO FEE
FEE.ORG/support

SUMMER SEMINARS
FEE.ORG/seminars

FOLLOW FEE
 feeonline @feeonline

"One night we asked people to blink their lights if they believed in freedom for Poland. We went to the window, and for hours, all of Warsaw was blinking."

This book is part of FEE's "Blinking Lights Project," which demonstrates the vital connection between good personal character and liberty.

Join the initiative at:

FEE.org/blinkinglights

Index

> "To suppose that any form of government will secure liberty or happiness without any virtue in the people, is a chimerical idea."
> —James Madison

"Bad character leads to bad policy and bad economics, which is bad for liberty," writes the author. "Without character, a free society is not just unlikely, it is impossible." This little book makes the case that character is indispensable for liberty, in America or anywhere else in the world.

Please consider giving copies of *Are We Good Enough for Liberty?* to students and teachers, local political leaders, business and labor associations, the news media, and to your activist friends all across America. Knowledge is power in political debate. This book will give you that power.

Special Bulk Copy Discount Schedule

1 book	$3.95	25 books	$50.00	500 books	$475.00
5 books	$17.00	50 books	$95.00	1000 books	$850.00
10 books	$27.00	100 books	$125.00		

All prices include postage and handling.

JAMESON BOOKS, INC   **ORDER TOLL FREE**
Post Office Box 738   **800-426-1357**
Ottawa, IL 61350

Please send me _____ copies of *Are We Good Enough for Liberty?*

Enclosed is my check for $ _____
or charge my [   ] MasterCard   [   ] Visa   [   ] Discover card:

No._____ Exp. Date_____

Signature_____
Telephone _____

Name_____
Address_____
City_____ State_____ Zip_____

Illinois residents please add 6.5% sales tax. Please allow 10 days for delivery.

> "To suppose that any form of government will secure liberty or happiness without any virtue in the people, is a chimerical idea."
>
> —James Madison

"Bad character leads to bad policy and bad economics, which is bad for liberty," writes the author. "Without character, a free society is not just unlikely, it is impossible." This little book makes the case that character is indispensable for liberty, in America or anywhere else in the world.

Please consider giving copies of *Are We Good Enough for Liberty?* to students and teachers, local political leaders, business and labor associations, the news media, and to your activist friends all across America. Knowledge is power in political debate. This book will give you that power.

Special Bulk Copy Discount Schedule

1 book	$3.95	25 books	$50.00	500 books	$475.00
5 books	$17.00	50 books	$95.00	1000 books	$850.00
10 books	$27.00	100 books	$125.00		

All prices include postage and handling.

JAMESON BOOKS, INC
Post Office Box 738
Ottawa, IL 61350

ORDER TOLL FREE
800-426-1357

Please send me _____ copies of *Are We Good Enough for Liberty?*

Enclosed is my check for $ _____
or charge my [　] MasterCard　[　] Visa　[　] Discover card:

No._____ Exp. Date_____

Signature_____
Telephone _____

Name_____
Address_____
City_____State_____Zip_____

Illinois residents please add 6.5% sales tax. Please allow 10 days for delivery.